PERTH A P(
TRAVEL GUIDE 2024

The ultimate Guide to Hidden Gems, Insider Tips, & Budget-Friendly Adventures (full-color travel guide)

DANIEL C. FLICK

Daniel C. Flick

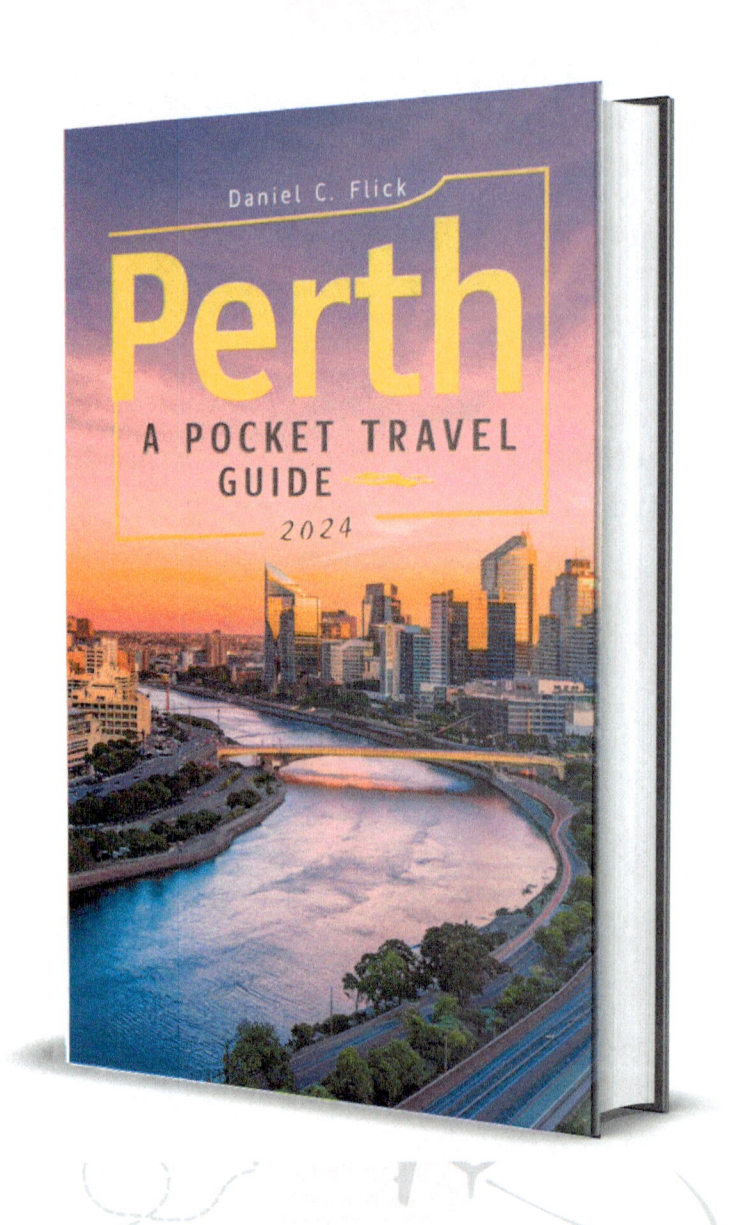

Perth
A POCKET TRAVEL GUIDE
2024

DANIEL C. FLICK

welcome to
PERTH

PERTH MAP

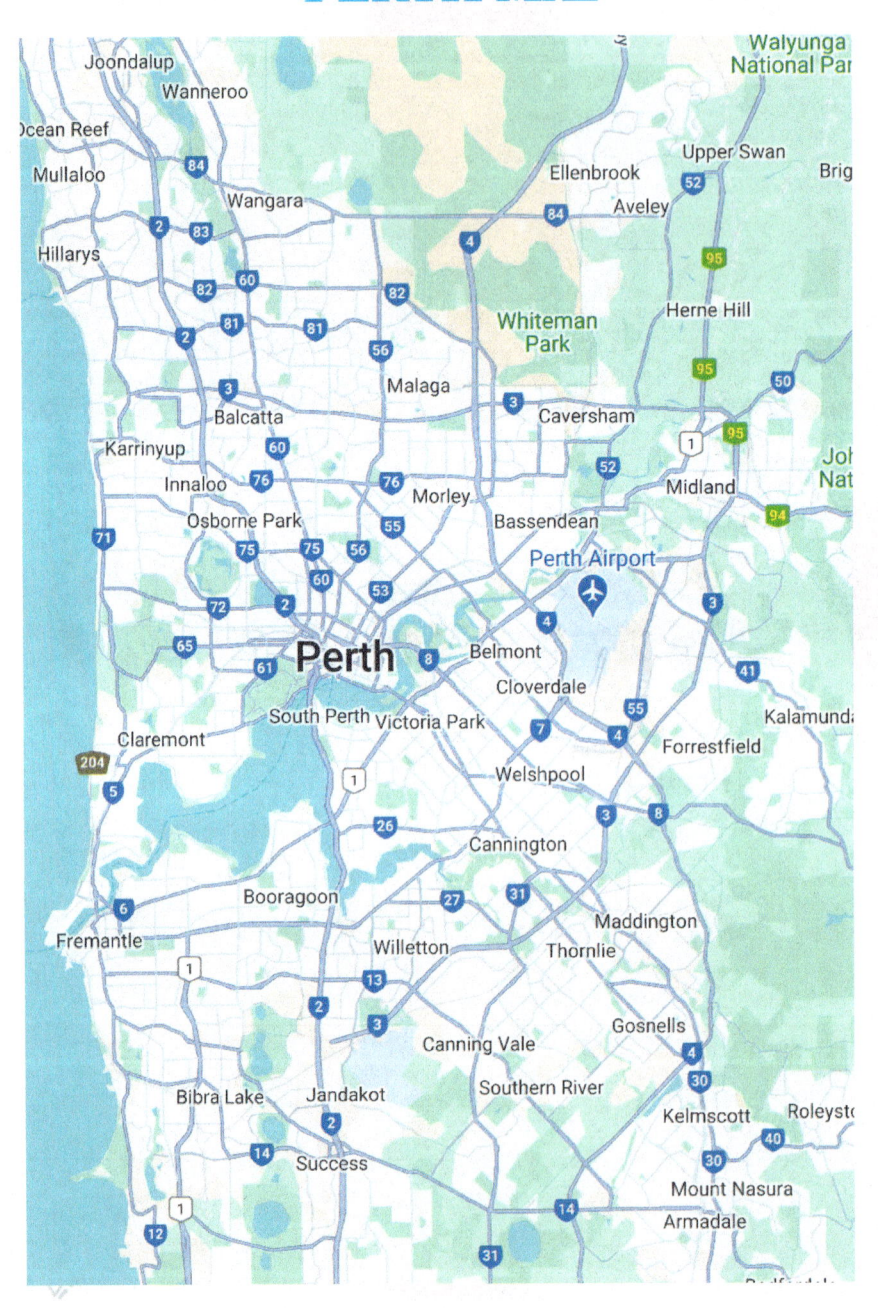

COPYRIGHT©2024 (DANIEL C. FLICK)
All intellectual property rights are retained. Without the express written permission of the publisher, no part of this book may be reproduced or transmitted in any form or by any means, electronic or mechanical, including photocopying, recording, or any information storing and retrieval system.

TABLE OF CONTENT

PERTH MAP _____ **5**

INTRODUCTION _____ **10**

ABOUT PERTH _____ **12**

   HISTORY AND CULTURE _____ 12

   GEOGRAPHY AND CLIMATE _____ 13

   WEATHER AND BEST TIME TO VISIT _____ 15

ARRIVAL IN PERTH _____ **17**

   GETTING TO PERTH _____ 17

   TRANSPORTATION OPTIONS: FROM THE AIRPORT TO CITY _____ 20

GETTING AROUND PERTH _____ **22**

   BUSES, TRAINS AND FERRIES _____ 22

   BIKING AND WALKING PATHS _____ 23

   TIPS FOR NAVIGATING THE CITY _____ 24

ACCOMMODATION _____ **25**

   LUXURY HOTELS AND RESORTS _____ 25

   BUDGET HOSTELS AND GUESTHOUSES _____ 27

   UNIQUE STAYS: BOUTIQUE AND HERITAGE ACCOMMODATIONS _ 28

EXPLORING PERTH _____ **30**

   KINGS PARK AND BOTANIC GARDEN _____ 30

   SWAN RIVER: CRUISES AND ACTIVITIES _____ 30

   PERTH CULTURAL CENTER _____ 31

   BEACHES AND COASTAL WALKS _____ 36

FREMANTLE: HISTORY AND MARITIME EXPLORATION	39
ROTTNEST ISLAND: QUOKKAS AND NATURAL BEAUTY	43

EATING OUT IN PERTH — *48*

INTRODUCTION TO PERTH'S CULINARY SCENE	48
TOP RESTAURANTS	51
COFFEE SHOPS AND CAFES	53
FOOD MARKETS	55

SHOPPING IN PERTH — *57*

SHOPPING DISTRICTS AND STREETS	57
MALLS AND SHOPPING CENTERS	59
ABORIGINAL ART AND SOUVENIRS	60

ENTERTAINMENT AND NIGHTLIFE — *64*

BARS, PUBS AND CLUBS	64
LIVE MUSIC AND PERFORMANCE VENUES	66
FAMILY-FRIENDLY ACTIVITIES	67

OUTDOOR ADVENTURES AND ACTIVITIES — *69*

PARKS AND GARDENS	69
HIKING AND BIKING TRAILS	73
WATER SPORTS AND BEACH ACTIVITIES	73
WILDLIFE ENCOUNTERS	74

DAY TRIPS FROM PERTH — *75*

PINNACLES DESERT	75
SWAN VALLEY: WINERIES AND WILDLIFE PARKS	76
MARGARET RIVER: WINE, SURF AND CAVES	78

NATIONAL PARKS AND NATURAL WONDERS	79
PRACTICAL INFORMATION FOR TRAVELERS	**81**
VISA AND ENTRY REQUIREMENTS	81
HEALTH AND SAFETY TIPS	81
CURRENCY, BANKING AND TIPPING	81
LOCAL CUSTOMS AND ETIQUETTE	82
COMMUNICATION: WI-FI, SIM CARDS AND APPS	82
EMERGENCY CONTACTS	83
CONCLUSION	**84**

INTRODUCTION

I had no idea what kind of experience awaited me when I got off the airport and saw Perth's bright sunshine. The voyage left a lasting impression on me, and the warmth and beauty of this far-off city on Australia's western coast will always be a part of me. Perth unfurled before me like a finely painted canvas, beckoning me to immerse myself in its rich textures and brilliant hues. It has immaculate beaches, boundless blue sky, and a bustling city life.

Perth whispered stories of its old land to me from the time I arrived. Here, the contemporary urban grazes the wildness, and the Swan River flows softly through, connecting the past and present. With their kind grins and easygoing manner, Perth's residents gave me the impression that I had returned home—a place I had never visited before. During these first days of discovery, I discovered that I was becoming deeply in love with the city.

Walking through the verdant Kings Park, one of the biggest inner-city parks in the world, with its stunning views of the city skyline and the peaceful river below, gave me a sense of awe every day. The park was a haven of peace and beauty with its natural bushland and floral gardens, demonstrating Perth's commitment to protecting its natural heritage.

The beaches of the city were yet another surprise. From the famous Cottesloe, with its turquoise seas and golden beaches, ideal for an orange and pink sunset paint job over the sky, to the surfer's haven at Scarborough Beach, every shoreline has a unique tale to tell, a song crafted by the waves calling out to me to sit and listen.

Perth's cultural landscapes are equally varied and rich. Theatricals, museums, and art galleries are rich sources of inspiration and creativity. The history of the city is interwoven throughout its streets, buildings, and public areas, spanning from its Indigenous origins to its European colonization and beyond. This encourages investigation and introspection.

Eating in Perth was an adventure in itself: every meal was a celebration of regional ingredients and creative cooking, a delectable mashup of tastes from all over the world. With each cup opening a new chapter in my Perth story, the city's passion for coffee carried me through quaint cafés and vibrant markets.

At the end of my tour, I came to the realization that Perth had given me much more than simply memories; it had given me tales to tell and recollections of places and people that would last long after I returned. This city had become a part of me, with its unending beauty, slow pace, and open heart.

If you're thinking of visiting Perth, know that you are about to go on an experience that will resonate deeply with your spirit. I welcome you to explore, travel, and fall in love with Perth as much as I did via these pages. Allow this guide to accompany you on your exploration of the captivating city that now harbors a little part of my heart. Welcome to Perth, where exploration and adventure await.

ABOUT PERTH

HISTORY AND CULTURE

Perth, the dynamic capital of Western Australia, has a rich cultural and historical legacy woven from its Indigenous roots, European colonization, and development into a global metropolis. Perth's history dates back to its indigenous Noongar people, who came to the city long before European immigrants did. For tens of thousands of years, the Noongar people have inhabited this territory and have maintained a close spiritual connection with their homeland, Boorloo, which is a part of the wider Whadjuk region.

Captain James Stirling established Perth as a component of the Swan River Colony in 1829, marking the beginning of the city's modern history. The community was founded as a free settler colony. It was named after Perth, Scotland, thanks to the influence of Sir George Murray, who was Secretary of State for War and the Colonies and a

Member of Parliament for Perthshire at the time. Perth's early growth and personality were greatly influenced by the fact that, in contrast to other Australian regions, it was not established as a convict colony.

Perth's sluggish but steady growth throughout the 19th century was facilitated by the Kalgoorlie region's gold discoveries in the late 1800s. The city saw tremendous growth and expansion as a result of the riches and migration surge generated by the gold rush. This boom era had a significant impact on the city's infrastructure, architecture, and society, laying the groundwork for Perth to become the metropolitan metropolis it is today.

Perth's culture is a patchwork of influences, shaped by the city's Indigenous history, British colonial past, and the many waves of immigrants who have called it home. Perth celebrates its cultural variety via its festivals, artwork, music, and cuisine. Perth International Arts Festival, Fringe World Festival, and Indigenous-led Perth Festival, which presents the world's oldest surviving cultures via music, dance, art, and storytelling, are just a few of the cultural events held in the city all year long.

The preservation of Indigenous historical and cultural places in and around Perth is another indication of respect for the land's original owners. One of the biggest inner-city parks in the world, Kings Park is home to Indigenous art and guided walks that tell the tales of the area's original occupants in addition to providing breathtaking vistas of the city. The Noongar people find cultural value in Kings Park.

The Western Australian Museum and the Art Gallery of Western Australia, two of Perth's museums and galleries, are essential to the preservation and exhibition of the city's history and cultural development. These institutions have collections that illustrate the rich history of the area and its people, ranging from current works to Indigenous art and artifacts.

Perth has a strong connection to its past even as it grows and changes. The history and culture of the city determine its identity and future; they are not just artifacts from the past. Perth is a tribute to the resilience and variety of its population, spanning from the Noongar people's age-old customs to the contemporary artistic manifestations of its citizens.

GEOGRAPHY AND CLIMATE

Contrasts characterize Perth's topography. The city opens out to the huge Indian Ocean to the west, where it is home to some of Australia's most stunning beaches, including Cottesloe Beach and Scarborough Beach, which are well-known for their smooth, white sand and crystal-clear blue seas. In addition to serving as a natural border to the east, the Darling Scarp offers a variety of outdoor pursuits, including hiking, bird viewing, and touring the national parks in the area.

Perth is located on the relatively flat Swan Coastal Plain, which the Swan River formed. The river itself serves as the center of the city, and parks, green spaces, and residential neighborhoods may be found along its banks. The river is an important aspect of city life since the major business area (CBD) of the city is located on its northern bank.

CLIMATE

Perth's climate is Mediterranean, with hot, dry summers and chilly, rainy winters. Perth has one of Australia's sunniest climates, with an average of around 3,200 hours of sunlight annually. The summertime temperature ranges from 17.5°C (63.5°F) to 30°C (86°F), with rare heatwaves causing temperatures to rise beyond 40°C (104°F). Perth residents spend a lot of time outside and at the beach throughout the summer because of the city's temperate climate and a steady supply of sunlight.

Perth has a moderate and rainy winter with average highs of 8°C (46.4°F) and lows of 19°C (66.2°F). This season's rains restore the natural environment by filling the region's streams and transforming the surrounding area into a lush, green setting. Winter days are frequently punctuated by bright, sunny moments despite the rain.

Seasonal wind patterns, including the well-known "Fremantle Doctor," a refreshing afternoon sea breeze that relieves summertime heat, also have an impact on Perth's climate. Particularly on steamy summer days, this natural air-conditioning system is a much-appreciated feature.

Perth's distinct topography and Mediterranean climate have greatly impacted the city's culture and way of life, promoting an outdoor-focused way of living. Both locals and tourists enjoy the stunning natural surroundings by participating in a variety of outdoor activities in the many parks and open spaces, such as sailing, cycling, and picnics.

WEATHER AND BEST TIME TO VISIT

September, October, or November are the ideal months to visit Perth since the city is filled with the vibrant hues and scents of spring, and there is little chance of rain during the bright days. Perth's summer months, December through February, are characterized by intense heat waves. The second-best time to go is most likely from March to May when the pleasant weather is ideal for outdoor activities like going to the beach. Here, June through August is considered a low season because of the cold weather and abundant rain in Perth.

From September until November

Perth is best visited in the spring when the flowers in Kings Park bloom and the calendar is full of activities, which is from September to November. This time of year, temperatures typically range from the mid-80s to the high 90s, but they have been known to hit 100 degrees. This time of year is when hotel rates are at their highest despite the scorching temperatures.

Important Occurrences:

September's Perth Royal Show
September's Listen Out Festival
September's Kings Park Festival
Western Australia Wine Show (October)

From December until February

Perth has its warmest months between December and February when highs above 100 degrees are common. Travelers may notice a small decrease in hotel costs from September to November despite the fact that the temperatures are starting to rise at this time of year.

Important Occurrences:

Australia Day (January) Skyworks
February–March: Perth International Arts Festival

March to May

Highs in the upper nineties mark Perth's autumnal months of March, April, and May, although they are less crowded than the city's peak months of September, October, and November. This is the best time to go if you're looking for a little dip in hotel rates and weather that's perfect for water sports.

Important Occurrences:

March Sculpture by the Sea

June to August

Perth has strong storms, a lot of rain, and 70s temps throughout the winter. Even with the pleasant temperatures, various water activities are often hindered during the rainy season. However, this is the time of year when hotel rates are at their lowest.

Important Occurrences:

July's Good Food and Wine Show

ARRIVAL IN PERTH

By AIR

First things first, you gotta snag a seat on a plane. and are your best bets. Play around with dates, be flexible, and keep your eyes peeled for deals.

Direct Flights or Layovers:
- Direct Flights: These are the dream, especially for long distances. Perth has direct flights from major cities in Asia, Europe, and the Middle East.
- Layovers: If direct flights aren't available, don't fret. There are plenty of options with one or two layovers, often in cities like Singapore, Kuala Lumpur, or Dubai.

Airline Choices:
- Major Airlines: Several big players like Emirates, Qatar Airways, and Singapore Airlines offer excellent service and connections to Perth.
- Budget Airlines: Airlines like Scoot and Jetstar might have cheaper fares, but be mindful of baggage fees and potential layovers.

Costs and Booking:

Prices can vary depending on the season, airline, and travel class. Here's a rough idea:

- Economy Class: Expect to pay anywhere from $800 to $2000 for a round-trip flight from major cities in the US, Europe, or Asia.

Pro Tip: Book your flights in advance, especially during peak seasons (summer in Australia is between December and February) to score the best deals.

Gear Up for the Journey:

- Passport: Make sure your passport has at least 6 months validity remaining from your travel date.
- Visa: Check visa requirements for Australia well in advance. You might need to apply online or visit the Australian embassy/consulate.
- Travel Insurance: Consider travel insurance to safeguard yourself against unexpected mishaps.

Luggage Blues:

- Check Baggage Allowance: Each airline has its own baggage allowance, so check their website beforehand to avoid hefty excess baggage fees.
- Pack Smart: Pack light and bring only essentials in your carry-on luggage. Liquids and gels must be in containers 3.4 ounces (100ml) or less and packed in a clear, resealable bag.

Airport Navigation:

- Arrive Early: Aim to reach the airport at least 3 hours before your international flight for check-in, security checks, and immigration.

- Check-in Online: Many airlines allow online check-in, saving you time at the airport. Download the airline's mobile app to breeze through the process.
- Security Breeze: Be prepared to have your belongings screened. Pack liquids and gels as per regulations.

Landing in Perth:
- Perth Airport: Perth Airport is the main entry point to Perth and Western Australia in general. Situated around 10 kilometers to the east of the city center, it has excellent connections to both domestic and foreign locations. Perth Airport is well-connected to the city center. You can hop on a taxi, rideshare service, or the train (recommended for budget-conscious travelers).

Bonus Tip:
- Download Entertainment: Long flights can get tedious. Pack your tablet or download movies/books to keep yourself entertained.

BY LAND

Traveling by land from Australia to Perth is a once-in-a-lifetime event for travelers. Whether you choose the romanticism of train travel or the majesty of the Australian outback, your trip will be epic.

Driving: From all around Australia, a network of roads connects Perth to other cities. Even though it's far from other big towns, driving there is a fantastic opportunity to see Australia's varied landscapes. The most well-known road is probably the Eyre Highway, which crosses the Nullarbor Plain and offers rewarding and difficult travel along with amazing scenery and uncommon animal encounters.

Rail: The Indian Pacific, which runs from Perth to Sydney via Adelaide, is one of the greatest rail rides in the world. The trip, which spans the whole continent of Australia, provides a broad perspective of the shifting climes of the nation, from the verdant Blue Mountains to the expansive deserts and brilliant wheat plains. With its opulent accommodations, fine food, and cozy sleeping cabins, it's a trip that will never be forgotten.

BY WATER

Due to its position on the Indian Ocean, Perth may also be reached by boat. The main port for this purpose is Fremantle Port, which is around a minute's drive from the city center. Fremantle is the port of entry for cruise ships and private yachts arriving from all over the globe, and it represents Perth's maritime gateway. The port town of Fremantle itself is a hive of activity, with a thriving cultural scene, fine dining choices, and a strong maritime heritage. When traveling by boat, visitors may take in Fremantle's relaxed atmosphere before seeing Perth and its environs' more extensive attractions.

TRANSPORTATION OPTIONS: FROM THE AIRPORT TO CITY

Train:
The Airport Line provides quick access to the city by connecting the airport with High Wycombe, East Perth, Perth, West Perth, and Claremont.
Redcliffe (near Terminals 3 and 4) and Airport Central (near Terminals 1 and 2) are the two rail stations that service the airport.

During peak hours, the Airport Line runs every 12 minutes; during off-peak hours, it runs every 15 minutes; at night, it runs every 30 minutes.

A single ticket costs around AUD 5.10, and the trip to the city center takes about 17 minutes from T3/T4 and 20 minutes from T1/T2.

Bus:

Bus route 292 links the terminals to Redcliffe Station, where passengers arriving by T3 or T4 may change to the Airport Line rail. Another alternative, albeit only on weekdays, is bus route 37, which runs from Airport Central Station to Oats Street Station.

Taxi:

Taxis are easily found at the airport, and it takes 20 to 25 minutes to get to the city center. A cab from the airport to the city center will run you around AUD 45.

Extra Details:

Perth Airport provides a convenient and quick means of accessing the city core and other locations, meeting a wide range of transportation demands. You will discover that the alternatives are accommodating, regardless of whether you prefer the ease of a cab or the speed of the rail.

Using a SmartRider card for public transportation may result in discounts for those seeking to save costs, including a 10% reduction on rail rates.

GETTING AROUND PERTH

BUSES, TRAINS AND FERRIES

Perth's free public Central Area Transit buses are the greatest means of transportation inside the city. Both rental vehicles and taxis are alternate options that may be arranged or summoned. But keep in mind that kilometers are used to measure distances and that Australians drive on the left side of the road. The city and its surroundings are too big to explore on foot, even if walking is one of the greatest methods to see the main sights. The popularity of biking has grown, and the adjacent port city of Fremantle even has a free bike-share program.

Less than ten miles east of the city center is Perth Airport (PER), where guests may arrive by air. Travelers arriving at the airport may use bus route No. 380, which goes to Elizabeth Quay and other rail and bus stops. From the airport, a cab journey to Perth's core business area would set you back AU$43, or around $33.

Bus

The free Central Area Transit buses, sometimes known as CATs, have four color-coded lines that travel looping circuits throughout Perth. Additionally, nearby cities like Fremantle and Joondalup provide free CATs. Although every route has its own set of hours, most start running between six and eight in the morning. And end operations between 6 and 8 p.m.

Cab

To reserve a taxi for a certain time, you may either phone ahead or hail one while driving (if the vehicle's light is on). There's also a taxi queue at 140 William Street, open from midnight until four in the morning and manned by security on Friday and Saturday evenings. If you would rather utilize a ridesharing service, Uber is also available in Perth.

Automobile

You may pick up your wheels at Perth Airport if you'd like them. But bear in mind that road signs with information on trip lengths and speed restrictions are posted in metric and that Australians drive on the left with the steering wheel on the right. To conduct a car in Western Australia, you do not need an international driving permit.

On Foot

Perth has a few walking locations, such as the Swan River and Kings Park & Botanical Garden, even if you can't get everywhere on foot.

By Motorcycle

Cycling is a well-liked and beautiful mode of transportation in Perth. One of the better routes follows the Swan River all the way to Elizabeth Quay and Narrows Bridge in East Perth, or it goes the other way to Garratt Road Bridge. The core business center of Perth is home to a number of bike rental stores, such as Cycle Center and About Bike Hire. Adult bike rentals start at AU$10 (about $7.50) for a full day.

BIKING AND WALKING PATHS

Perth is the perfect destination for recreational and mountain bikers due to its extensive network of cycle and dual-use trails that stretch from the city center to surrounding areas. Popular routes with distinctive landscapes and experiences include the Swan Valley Cycle Trails, Fremantle Cycle Trails, Perth Beaches Cycle Trails, and Perth City Cycle Trails. Bicycle tours and rentals are easily accessible for individuals who want to explore the city, the Swan River, Fremantle, and Rottnest Island.

Perth's riverfront bike paths are well-marked for anyone looking for a bike-friendly urban experience. Metropolitan bicycle businesses also provide thorough cycle maps. Numerous bike rental alternatives are available from establishments, including Spinway WA at Kings Park and About Bike Hire at Point Fraser. One of the most famous cycling routes is the River Loop Cycle, which passes by a number of Swan River bridges as well as parks, eateries, and cafés.

Emphasized Paths

- Kings Park has a variety of bike routes through native Australian bushland, as well as expansive vistas.
- For those who like the great outdoors, the 41-kilometer Railway Reserves Heritage Trail circles Perth's national parks.
- The 27-kilometer City Cycle Trail circles some of Perth's most notable city landmarks, such as Elizabeth Quay and Kings Park.
- The Swan River Three Bridges Loop offers a 43km alternative for experienced riders, catering to riders of all skill levels.

TIPS FOR NAVIGATING THE CITY

Keep Left, Stay Alert: Unless you are passing, always stay to the left and be vigilant, particularly at night or while using headphones.

Use Your Bell: Cyclists should indicate their intention to pass other path users by sounding their bell.

Bicyclists must yield to pedestrians on shared pathways, especially those using motorized wheelchairs or mobility scooters.

Path etiquette: If you see an animal or youngster, slow down and move off the path. Observe all posted signage and traffic controller instructions about closures and diversions

ACCOMMODATION

LUXURY HOTELS AND RESORTS

1. Perth's The Ritz-Carlton

Situated along the Swan River, this opulent hotel on 1 Barrack Street offers expansive views of Perth's skyline. It has an on-site spa, a cutting-edge fitness facility, and an outdoor infinity pool. The Ritz-Carlton is a great place for both business and leisure tourists because of its large conference rooms and exquisite wedding venues. You should budget around $70 for parking on the property. They also provide limousine and private vehicle services for those seeking more opulent travel.

2. Perth's Crown Towers

As the first officially designated 6-star hotel in Perth, Crown Towers is well-known for its abundant lodging choices, which include the Chairman's Villa, which is valued at over $25,000 per night. Standard accommodation prices begin at around $400. As a component of the Crown complex, this resort provides guests with access to a theater, casino, and a variety of eating establishments, including Nobu and Rockpool Bar & Grill. The hotel has large lagoon pools and luxurious accommodations with stunning views of the city skyline and Swan River.

3. Perth's Westin
The Westin, which is centrally located downtown Perth, is well-known for its plentiful lodgings and consistently receives high marks from visitors. With its sleek accommodations, cutting-edge facilities, and dedicated service, it guarantees an amazing stay. The hotel is a perfect option for experiencing Perth because of its accessible location, which provides easy access to city center attractions.

4. Perth City Centre InterContinental
With its opulent accommodations, attentive service, and expansive city views, this hotel provides an elegant urban hideaway. Every day, the Club InterContinental offers a unique experience that includes a la carte breakfast, refreshments throughout the day, and evening beverages. Its ideal location makes it more appealing to visitors looking for convenience and elegance.

5. QT Perth
With on-site restaurants and fitness centers, QT Perth is a designer hotel in the heart of the city, perfect for those who value the finer things in life. The hotel guarantees a great stay with its unique décor

and first-rate customer service. Luxurious accommodations with stunning bathrooms and smart TVs can be found at QT Perth.

6. COMO Treasury
COMO The Treasury, a premium destination in Perth's central business district, is housed in exquisitely renovated mid-19th-century buildings and has received an amazing 9.6 rating from visitors. Well-known for its healthy food selections and outstanding service, this hotel offers large, tastefully decorated rooms that provide for a peaceful urban retreat. Because of its convenient location, seeing Perth's top sights is a snap.

BUDGET HOSTELS AND GUESTHOUSES

1. Billabong Backpackers Resort: This hostel in Perth has a tour desk, internet café, laundry facilities, and a front desk open around the clock, among other services. Its clean, well-maintained rooms and pleasant personnel have earned it recognition. Nightly rates begin at around £57.

2. The Emperor's Crown Hostel: With both dorm rooms and private choices, this spotless and contemporary hostel welcomes backpackers, students, and budget travelers and is just five minutes from Perth's central business district. It is a cozy and practical option with a fully furnished kitchen, free WiFi in public areas, and plenty of sitting spots.

3. Pensione Hotel: With hotel rates beginning at €84 per night, the Pensione Hotel is a budget-friendly, spotless, and cozy choice for travelers seeking lodging in Perth's central business district. Its

amenities include fast Wi-Fi, ensuite bathrooms, and very comfy mattresses. The hotel's convenient location makes it simple to go to a variety of food establishments.

4. Fremantle jail YHA: Housed within the world heritage-listed Fremantle Prison structure, this unusual hostel gives visitors the option of sleeping in former jail cells. Prices for private rooms and dormitories start at €19 per bed in a dorm with ten beds. The beach and Fremantle Markets are just a short distance away.

5. Dunsborough Beachouse YHA: This hostel is close to Geographe Bay Beach and charges €25.39 for a 6-bed dorm. It's a fantastic starting point for outdoor pursuits, including beach and cave exploration, table tennis, and volleyball. In the nights, the hostel becomes a bustling place that's ideal for those who want to meet new people.

UNIQUE STAYS: BOUTIQUE AND HERITAGE ACCOMMODATIONS

1. Perth's Quay:
The tiny but exquisite accommodations of the Esplanade Studio rooms of this boutique hotel located at 18 The Esplanade, Perth, WA 6000, are sure to make an impression. The Louis T Collection's Quay Perth enthralls with its earthy tones, Victorian ash wood, and comfortable, luxurious furniture. It's a fantastic option for both pleasure and business visitors because of its noteworthy amenities, which include bathtubs, bay window chairs, and a co-working room open 24/7. The mid-range prices give value with a distinct flare.

2. The Hotel Alex:
Located in Northbridge, the center of Perth's culture and entertainment, The Alex Hotel caters to those seeking a boutique hotel experience that prioritizes comfort and simplicity. The rooms are carefully designed, with amenities and local brands, and come in a range of sizes to suit the demands of every kind of guest. The hotel takes great pleasure in its public living areas, which promote relaxation and socialization among its guests. Highlights include a rooftop patio and the hotel's proximity to a bustling nightlife, which makes it the perfect option for those wishing to experience Perth's energetic vibe fully.

3. Perth Tribe:
With its inventive design, Tribe Perth redefines the conventional hotel experience. It is made up of 63 prefabricated containers that are combined to provide a distinctive and contemporary lodging alternative in West Perth. The hotel's philosophy is on designing public areas with the needs of its guests in mind and eliminating extras for a more practical and economical stay. It's a great choice for those looking for a modern, stylish setting that's yet conveniently close to Perth's central business district.

4. The Hotel National:
Located in the bustling center of Fremantle, The National Hotel provides a distinctive stay in a tastefully renovated historic structure. This lodging is renowned for its amazing fusion of historical details and contemporary elegance, with each room reflecting the original charm of the building in addition to modern amenities. The hotel is the ideal location for anybody wishing to enjoy the rich cultural and historical heritage of Fremantle because of its breathtaking views of

the city and its port. The National Hotel offers a trip into the past with all the conveniences of the present, not simply a place to stay.

EXPLORING PERTH

KINGS PARK AND BOTANIC GARDEN

Among the greatest parks in the world, Kings Park & Botanic Garden may compete with Central Park in New York, El Retiro in Madrid, and Stanley Park in Vancouver. In addition to the more than 3,000 different types of trees and plants found in the park's numerous sections—from red-flowering gum trees in the Fraser Avenue Precinct to flora, wildlife, and fungus unique to bushland—there are playgrounds, playing fields, cafés, and picnic spots. In addition, the park's Rio Tinto Naturescape, which is scheduled to open in 2018, will include areas for rock climbing and scrambling in addition to a stream for paddling and a wading area.

The wide walking routes in this park are a favorite among both tourists and residents, drawing in a diverse range of visitors, including families and seniors. Others claim that the wind and shade on hot summer days, together with the city vistas from the strolling paths—

particularly the elevated Lotterywest Federation Walkway—are just "fabulous."

The Kings Park & Botanic Garden is free to access and open around the clock. It's located across the Swan River from the zoo in Perth.

SWAN RIVER: CRUISES AND ACTIVITIES

Some time spent in or near Swan River is essential, whether you cycle or stroll by it to go to Elizabeth Quay or float along on a boat to the port city of Fremantle. Swan River offers several river cruises from businesses like Captain Cook Cruises, cycling lanes, and walking trails. It's a lovely way to see the city and get to all of its attractions. For usage in and near Swan River, visitors may also hire bikes from About Bike Hire, paddleboards from Funcats, and kayaks from Rivergods.

Reviews on the best method to see the Swan River differ among travelers. Some propose taking a river cruise to Fremantle, while others advise going for an early stroll before the noon heat arrives. Though the establishments that rent out equipment have defined

hours, visitors may enjoy the Swan River year-round. Some describe the experience of watching the sunset and
the stars rise as "magical."

PERTH CULTURAL CENTER

The arts, culture, knowledge, and community are all brought together at the Perth Cultural Centre.

The city's cultural center is a place to take in the sunlight, utilize the free WiFi, and participate in the activities schedule and Perth events.

Situated near public transportation and serving as a critical link between Northbridge's retail, food and beverage, and entertainment zone and the Perth CBD, the Cultural Centre has seen a metamorphosis from an underutilized area to a vibrant public place.

The Perth Cultural Centre is home to the major educational, cultural, and artistic institutions in the State, such as:

Western Australian Art Gallery

Museum of Western Australia

Western Australian State Library

The Perth Institute of Contemporary Arts

The Blue Room Theatre

Western Australia's State Theatre Centre

State Records Office of the Central Institute of Technology

Perth Cultural Centre Play space

which emphasizes sensory play. The Perth Cultural Centre Playspace blends art and nature with interactive elements that children may handle and investigate, such as rotating wheels and wood sculptures. Perfectly crafted with organic hues and textures, it exudes a serene vibe even in the heart of the metropolis.

Whereabouts
Street Corner of James and William
Perth, Western Australia 6000

Boola Bardip, WA Museum

The many tales of Western Australia may be shared at the WA Museum Boola Bardip.
their roles in the world, people, and locations. Boola Bardip is Nyoongar for "many stories," the name of the country the museum is located in.

The Museum contains eight permanent galleries, each with a unique subject and set of exhibits that were created after consulting with almost 54,000 residents of Western Australia.

A 1,000 square meter special exhibition gallery, five magnificent heritage-listed buildings, shop and café areas, and, of course, hundreds of objects from the State's collections presented in creative and original ways are all features of the WA Museum Boola Bardip.

WA Museum Boola Bardip is a venue for amusement, education, discussion, and creativity.

Discover the histories and customs of the local Aboriginal population as well as the viewpoints of the people and groups who have influenced the identity and feeling of place of Western Australia.

Otto, the 24-meter blue whale skeleton, fossils and replicas of the unique flora, animals, and amazing land formations of the State, intriguing minerals and meteorites, and the megafauna and dinosaurs that once roamed ancient Earth are some of the highlights of the museum. Don't forget to take a selfie at the museum using the crystal gateway.

Everyday hours for the Museum are 9.30 a.m. to 5 p.m.

Whereabouts
James Street
Northbridge, Washington, US 6000

Gallery Central
Gallery Central at North Metro TAFE features art that feeds the creative spirit and broadens the intellect.
In addition to offering art lessons and an Artist-in-Residence program, Gallery Central has many art spaces.
Its shows, held in a beautifully furnished and conveniently situated Creative Industries teaching facility, are approachable and topical, appealing to a broad audience.

Gallery Central features a variety of artists, including faculty, students, and alums from the college on occasion.
Visual arts, jewelry, pottery, fashion and textiles, graphic design, interior design and decorating, design for industry, photography, film and TV, music, animation, and multimedia are among the subjects taught at North Metro TAFE.

The Gallery is open every day except Christmas Day, Good Friday, and Tuesdays. All ages are welcome, and contributions are accepted. Certain special exhibits could need reservations.
Whereabouts
Perth Cultural Center
Perth, Western Australia 6000
Operating Hours
Wednesday–Monday, 10 a.m.–5 p.m.; closed on Tuesdays, Good Friday, and Christmas Day.
There is no charge to enter the gallery.

The Performing Arts Museum

If you have a fondness for theater and collectibles... then go straight to the Museum of Performing Arts for an enlightening look at the history of theater.

His Majesty's Theatre has featured a wide range of entertainment genres during its colorful and fascinating history, including vaudeville, stand-up comedy, ballet, modern dance, opera, musical theater, and much more.

In 2001, His Majesty's Theatre inaugurated the Museum of Performing Arts as a tribute to its illustrious past.

Every six to eight weeks, a new exhibition with objects such as spectacular costumes, pictures, newspaper clippings, screenplays, scores, and other historical artifacts is available for public viewing at the Museum below at the Maj.

The earliest artifact in the Museum's collection is a stunning silk program from an amateur theatrical production in Perth that was created in 1854.

Whereabouts
Hay Street, 825
Perth, Western Australia 6000

Operating Hours
Weekdays: 10 a.m. to 4 p.m.
Closed on Saturday and Sunday

Museum of the Royal Perth Hospital

From the hospital's founding in 1855 to the present, the Royal Perth Hospital Museum takes visitors on a colorful tour of its history.

Despite alterations and enlargements, the original Colonial Hospital structure remains at the intersection of Murray Street and Victoria Square.

The 1894 Administration Building, which once housed nurse's and matron's quarters, a dispensary, an outpatient surgery center, and consultation rooms, is home to the museum and is just next door.

The historical medical equipment offers an interesting window into Perth's social growth as well as the ongoing developments in the medical and healthcare industries.

Early surgical and anesthetic tools, nursing uniforms, pictures, an iron lung, and early educational aids are all part of the collection.

A box that holds Australia's first X-ray machine is one of the museum's most prized artifacts. The Cold Cathode X-ray tubes were brought in from France by Dr. W. J. Hancock to aid in patient examinations in the early 1900s.

The goal of the museum is to promote understanding of the past of the hospital that has served Washington state for the longest and is well-known for its innovative and excellent contributions to patient care, medical research, and education.

Whereabouts

Ground Floor, Block M, 10–14 Murray Street

Perth, Western Australia 6000

Operating Hours

Thursday and Wednesday, 9 a.m. to 2 p.m.

King Street Arts Center

The King Street Arts Centre is a place where dance, theater, culture, and art all come together.

The Center is housed in the historic Munster House and is situated in Perth between King and Murray Streets.

Munster House, which was first constructed in the early 1900s, underwent a major renovation in the late 1990s to become the King Street Arts Center.

The West Australian Youth Theatre Company (WAYTC), Performing Arts, Perth Centre of Photography, The Last Great Hunt, CO3, Community Arts Network WA (CANWA), Regional Arts WA, Sensorium Theatre, and the Last Great Hunt are among the tenants.

Private corporations and arts organizations may reserve both of the King Street Art Centre's two conference rooms.

Whereabouts

357–365 Murray Street, Perth; King St. and Munster Lane are the entrance points.

Perth, Western Australia 6000

Operating Hours

All seven days a week from 8:00 am to 9:00 pm, the three Studios and the large and small conference rooms are for rent.

BEACHES AND COASTAL WALKS

The coastal stroll paths in Perth provide a variety of experiences by combining natural beauty with a historical past. Take a trip along the Yanchep National Park Ghost House Walk to see Western Australia's beautiful natural surroundings, where you may explore lush woods and see local species. The Indian Ocean and cityscape may be seen in breathtaking panoramic views from the Reabold Hill Summit Boardwalk. The Mosman Park Heritage Trail offers stories of the region's past as it winds through significant historical sites, catering to history enthusiasts. Perth provides walkers of all interests with the ideal combination of outdoor adventure and cultural discovery with its variety of coastline and history paths.

Boardwalk at Reabold Hill Summit

200 meters; five minutes; easy difficulty

Reabold Hill, which is situated in Bold Park, Floreat, is the metro area's highest natural point on the Swan Coastal Plain and, at 85 meters, provides expansive views over Perth, the Indian Ocean, and the Darling Scarp. With its elevated boardwalk, lounging areas, artwork, and bird life, visitors may fully immerse themselves in the wilderness experience.

The Heritage Trail in Mosman Park

10.5 kilometers; 3 to 4 hours; Easy to Moderate difficulty

Discover some of the historical attractions of Mosman Park and the hints that have been left behind by taking a stroll along the Mosman Park Heritage Trail. The route travels down the river, into the wilderness, and back into the center of Mosman Park, stopping at sixteen different locations. Spend some time exploring the route, and don't forget to enjoy the stunning surroundings of this unusual town, which is located between a river and the sea.

Yaberoo Budjara Historical Path

28 kilometers; several days; moderate difficulty

This 28-kilometer, one-way route in Wanneroo City is inspired by Yellagonga and his people's journey between Yanchep and Lake Joondalup. It may be finished in chunks. It stretches over tuart and banksia woods, coastal heath, and former wetlands from Neil Hawkins Park in the south to Yanchep National Park in the north. It is accessible in the following parts and has red markers with a grasstree symbol.

Hester Avenue to Neil Hawkin's Park: This area was once a stock path. The word "the lake that glistens" refers to Lake Joondalup, a large freshwater body that the Aboriginal people highly prized as a location for hunting and camping. While tuart, marri, and parrot bush are widespread on the western side of the route, paperbark and seashore vegetation predominate on the eastern side. The path uses former quarry access roads to enter Neerabup National Park. There are views of the Indian Ocean from the top of the peak.

The track continues through jarrah and sheoak on Hester Ave. to Romeo Road in Neerabup National Park. After that, the low banksia woods give way to the coastal limestone heath. There are vistas in all directions from the summit of the limestone ridge.

Romeo Road to Yanchep National Park: The track continues near Wanneroo Road, but plant invasion and fire have badly damaged this region. After there, it enters Yanchep National Park and goes via Pipidinny Swamp. To the west is a sizable grove of tuarts. The trail meanders close to Loch McNess until it enters Yanchep National Park. This region was historically used for rituals, meetings, and corroboration.

FREMANTLE: HISTORY AND MARITIME EXPLORATION

Fremantle is rich in history, ranging from the first maritime excursion to the old port structures.

Australian West Indies

Fremantle's Maritime Museum

Situated at the meeting point between Fremantle and the ocean, the world-class WA Nautical Museum tells the narrative of Western Australia's maritime heritage.

Immerse yourself in the deep experiences of Western Australia's early ocean explorers and the maritime history that has contributed to the creation of our magnificent state by visiting the recently opened Western Australian Maritime Museum on Victoria Quay in Fremantle. The America's Cup-winning boat Australia II, owned by Alan Bond, and six themed exhibitions are housed in this iconic building:

The Indian Ocean

Australia via Tin Canoe II

Swan River and Fremantle

Addiction to Fishing

Transports

Navy Defense

Millions of people have arrived in Western Australia by ocean liner, steamer, sailing ship, and military vessel while traveling to other Australian ports or as immigrants hoping to settle in Western Australia. Australia's population is quite diversified in terms of culture because of immigration from all over the globe. An essential part of this history is the Port of Fremantle.

OPEN: 9:30 to 5:00 every day

Observed holidays are Good Friday, Easter Monday, Anzac Day, Christmas Day, Boxing Day, and New Year's Day.

ENTRANCE FEES: $15.00 for adults, FREE for children aged 5 to 15, $7.50 for concessions, and $15.00 for family entry (up to two adults and three children).

Displaying an Oberon Class former Royal Australian Navy submarine,

HMAS Ovens

HMAS Ovens, an Oberon class submarine that was once in the Royal Australian Navy (RAN), is accessible for excursions and is situated next to the Maritime Museum. She was the first submarine to be kept intact and turned into a museum ship in Australia.

You can imagine what it would have been like to be on board this magnificent ship during the Cold War. Being a submariner is not as glamorous as you may believe. Every time they go below the ocean's surface, they endanger their lives.

The Scott Shipbuilding and Engineering Company in Greenock, Scotland, constructed this Oberon Class vessel. With a submerged speed of more than 15 knots, HMAS Ovens is 89.9 meters in length. With the motto "Silence is Golden," she was launched at Greenock on December 4, 1967. She was put into service on April 18, 1969, and made her first journey to Australia, arriving in Sydney on October 17, 1969.

OPEN: Daily tours run for one hour every thirty minutes, from 10:00 am to 4:30 pm.

Observed holidays are Good Friday, Easter Monday, Anzac Day, Christmas Day, Boxing Day, and New Year's Day.

Admission Fees: $15.00 for adults, $7.50 for children aged 5 to 15, $7.50 for concessions, and $40.00 for family entry (up to two adults and three children). There are annual passes available. Because the tour is popular, get your tickets in advance.

The Round House, which was once Fremantle Prison

Originally constructed in 1831, the Round House is the oldest surviving public structure in Western Australia. Up until 1886, it served as a prison or jail when it was constructed.

It had a jailer's apartment and eight cells that led onto a central courtyard. Later on, the head constable, his wife, and their ten kids lived there. It is now a well-liked tourist destination with expansive vistas.

The Round House is situated in the Arthur Head Precinct, in what is now known as Fremantle's West End, on a peninsula with unobstructed views of Cockburn Sound and the river mouth. The courthouse, residences, and two lighthouses were among the other structures located atop Arthur Head.

Every day, the Volunteer Heritage Guides (FVHG) of Fremantle hoist the flags and take part in the cannon fire at one o'clock. In the early 1900s, this technique was used as a means of maintaining 'order' in the growing colony by keeping everyone's timepieces synchronized.

The marine chronometer, invented by English clockmaker John Harrison, was the first to overcome the problem of keeping clocks "in time." It allowed ships at sea to "carry" the proper time with them even after they lost sight (and sound) of the coast.

10 Arthur Head, Fremantle, WA, 6160 is the address.

OPEN: Daily, 10.30 a.m. to 3.30 p.m.
Good Friday and Christmas Day are CLOSED.

Admission Fees: Donation-based.

You can view the Indian Ocean from the Round House. On the left, you can see Bathers Beach behind the cliffs, while on the right, you can see cruise ships entering the harbor! Fantastic.

Fremantle Prison

The 2011 Western Australian Heritage Awards went to the Fremantle Prison for:

Extraordinary Input from Organizations, Public and Private Excellent Product for Heritage Tourism.

The Terrace in Fremantle, Western Australia, is home to the old Australian jail known as "Fremantle Prison." It is situated about 200 meters east of the Fremantle Markets.

The jail, gatehouse, surrounding walls, cottages, tunnels, and prisoner art are all located on the 60,000 m² (15 acres) property. Convict labor was used to construct the imposing prison, which was turned over to the colonial authorities in 1886 to serve as a Fremantle Gaol (Fremantle Prison) for inmates with local sentences. It's no longer a jail, despite its name, the 'Fremantle jail.'

OPEN: Every day. The public may see prisoner art in the Prison Gallery, which is open every day from 10:00 am to 5:00 pm. There is no charge to enter the gallery. Christmas Day and Good Friday are CLOSED. The gatehouse, visitor center, prison gallery, gift shop, and convict cafe all provide free admission.

ROTTNEST ISLAND: QUOKKAS AND NATURAL BEAUTY

The sunny vacation island of Rottnest / Wadjemup is located only 20 km off the coast of Fremantle, yet it seems like a world away. It is endowed with a laid-back vibe, gorgeous landscape, vibrant marine life, and some of the best beaches and pristine bays on the planet. The island is known by its Noongar name, Wadjemup, which translates to "place across the water where the spirits are." The Whadjuk Noongar people, the land's original owners, see the island as both a place of remembrance for the Aboriginal men and boys whose remains still lie under Wadjemup's sands and a place where spirits rest. We recognize and honor the history of our country.

Encircled by the vast Indian Ocean, Rottnest Island boasts empty beaches and pedestrian-only streets and is the natural habitat of the globally recognized quokkas. You may explore the beaches and bays and enjoy the sunlight, waves, and snorkeling—these are the things that make vacations magical.

With so many excursions, events, and attractions available on Rottnest Island, you won't be short of things to do. Take a Segway tour, jump off the beach, or assemble to hear Wadjemup Aboriginal legends. Railways, museums, lighthouses, barracks, and artifacts from the conflict all illustrate the more recent past. See the pastel sunset silhouette boats on the bay. Enjoy wine and seafood at bars along the shore, or pick up a "craydog" from The Lane. Visit for a day, stay for a week. Here, the shoreline settings provide the background for your enduring recollections.

Activities on the Island of Rottnest

Are you unsure about what to do on Rottnest Island? Here are some of the top choices.

You have 63 beaches and 20 bays to select from where you may swim and unwind by the gorgeous seas.

Savor an opulent seafood cruise with all the trimmings, from the sea to the plate.

Take an adventurous boat cruise for 90 minutes from September to April.

At Little Salmon Bay, explore underwater snorkeling and marine life.

See every must-see place on Rottnest Island via bus tour.

While trekking along the Wadjemup Bidi, stray off the trail.

Experience a range of flora and fauna, such as wildflowers, quokkas, and birds.

Take one of the island's numerous complimentary walking excursions led by a guide.

Take a sunset catamaran cruise or explore the bays on Charter 1's snorkeling trip.

Take a parasailing adventure with Cicerellos Jet Adventures and soar to new heights.

Visit the Wadjemup Museum to discover more about the island's past.

Take a walking tour of the island with a Noongar guide to learn about it from the Aboriginal viewpoint.

Accessing and Navigating Rottnest Island

Rottnest Express, Rottnest Fast Ferries, and SeaLink Rottnest Island provide quick ferry rides to Rottnest Island from Fremantle, Perth City, and Hillarys. Additionally, Kookaburra Air, Rottnest Air-Taxi, Corsaire Aviation, and Swan River Seaplanes are available for flights.

Bicycles are the best mode of transportation for exploring Rottnest Island; you may rent them or bring them with you when you go by boat. The island is simple to visit, with many wonderful routes to take once you arrive. It is just 11 km long and 4.5 km wide. If riding a bike seems like more work, you may take the Island Explorer, an air-conditioned bus that will transport you there. There are 18 stations on the schedule for this daily hop-on/hop-off service. Alternatively, you may reserve a seat for the recently introduced, simple, on-demand Rottnest Water-Taxi service. Many of the remote harbors and well-kept secrets on the island are visited by the excursion. Bicycles and buses are other ways to get about the island. Just cycle till you're exhausted, then drop it off at a bus stop and take the bus back to the village. This is perfect for novice cyclists or families.

You may reserve a variety of excursions at the tourist center. A vintage train ride, lighthouse tours, snorkeling excursions, Segway tours, skydiving, and photography trips are among the options.

A Water Play Area

Are you still pondering your plans for Rottnest Island? Unsurprisingly, being near water is a big part of island life—from swimming and snorkeling to fishing, surfing, boating, and sailing! Diving beneath the surface is a genuinely rewarding experience, replete with colorful tropical fish and coral. The world's most southerly corals can be found on Rottnest Island, and experienced divers will be pleased to learn that a huge cemetery of shipwrecks lies just off the coast, just waiting to be discovered. There are informational plaques next to the wrecks, and for those who would rather not venture down to the deep end, there are also plaques onshore that show where the wrecks are.

Additionally well-known for its surfing, Strickland Bay on Rottnest Island boasts some of the world's best breaks. The best months to go surfing are May through
October.

What to eat on Rottnest Island

You'll have plenty of options when it comes to food and beverages. Savor locally inspired meals at Pinky's Rottnest Island, dine on the beach and indulge in fresh seafood at Isola Bar e Cibo, or go on a Southeast Asian culinary adventure at Lontara. Enjoy excellent coffee at The Lane, Dome Café, and Geordie's Café. If you're in the mood for some delectable pub fare, visit Hotel Rottnest. Snack on something light from The General Store, Subway, Frankies on Rotto, and Rottnest Bakery.

Engage with Wildlife and the Environment

There are several walking and cycling routes on Rottnest Island; once you get off the boat, you may pick up a map from the tourist center. You will travel through breathtaking lakes, magnificent coastline headlands, and both artificial and natural wonders along the Wadjemup Bidi. The 45 kilometers of trails that make up Wadjemup Bidi are divided into five parts, each of which has noteworthy historical and natural sites to see and explore.

Beginners and experienced hikers alike may enjoy pack-free, luxury adventure walking excursions on Rottnest Island with The Hike Collective, an all-inclusive eco-tour. Paul's Eco E-bike Tours offers electric bike tours that take you to some of the most picturesque spots on the island. On an electric bike tour, you will ride beside an experienced guide, stroll along the beach, or swim in one of the many stunning beaches.

Study the history and culture of the Aboriginal people.
Learn more about the distinctive island by taking part in one of the Rottnest Island Volunteer Guides' free guided walking excursions. Learn more and heighten your appreciation for Wadjemup on a walking tour with the award-winning Go Cultural Aboriginal Tours & Experiences.

EATING OUT IN PERTH

INTRODUCTION TO PERTH'S CULINARY SCENE

Although not as established as Sydney or Melbourne, Perth is quickly becoming one of Australia's top gourmet destinations. Its closeness to the Indian Ocean means eateries have access to loads of fresh seafood, as well as typical Australian staples like steak and lamb. Western Australia is the nation's biggest wheat producer, too. Perth's best foods span from the familiar, like sourdough bread, to Aussie classics to the more exotic, like kangaroo.

Rock Lobster

The Western rock lobster (sometimes known as crayfish) is Western Australia's most renowned seafood. In Cervantes, a two-hour drive north of Perth, you can eat rock lobster right from the boat, but you'll also be able to get it in the city.

Try Joe's Fish Shack near the Fremantle fishing boat port or The Cray in Belmont for fresh local lobster. Like other areas throughout the globe, Western Australian rock lobster doesn't come cheap. Be prepared to spend at least US$40 for a whole lobster at a restaurant.

Meat pie

Meat pies are quintessential Australian fare, and Perth produces some particularly excellent interpretations of this classic meal. You may experiment with tastes like mushrooms, poultry, mashed potato, or even cheese and bacon after you've had the traditional beef and pastry version.

Pasta

Fremantle, Australia's westernmost port, used to be the first point of call for European immigrants traveling to Australia. Thousands of Italian immigrants settled in Perth during World War II, bringing with them the skills necessary to start a regional pasta craze.

Purists of fresh pasta will be pleased with Lulu La Delizia in Subiaco. The six-course seasonal tasting menu at Lalla Rookh is a must-try, and Garum is renowned for pairing excellent local meats with delicious pasta prepared in the Roman way.

Barracuda

Asiatic seabass, or barramundi, is indigenous to Australia and the Indo-Pacific region. Even the most anti-seafood customers like the mild taste and minimal fat content of the white flesh. It's often served grilled in Perth, with a lovely crispy skin.

Excellent local fillets may be found at Sweetlips Fish Bar (Scarborough and Melville), while W Churchill in the city center serves delicious crispy skin barramundi.

Sourdough bread

Perth has a remarkable array of artisan bakeries that maximize the use of regional wheat. The sourdough movement has completely taken over the city, and almost every café serves freshly baked bread with creative toppings.

While Chu Bakery in Highgate specializes in toast and sweet delights, Bread in Common in Fremantle serves up easy and excellent sandwiches, cheeses, and sharing plates. Subiaco's Sorganic is the place to go for baguettes and breakfast.

kangaroo

Australia has more kangaroos than humans, and if you visit Western Australia, you can see a few of them jumping about in the countryside. You can get kangaroo meat in a lot of stores and restaurants if you'd want to try one too. A common description of the meat is that it tastes like an extremely lean cut of beef.

Furthermore, kangaroo meat is inexpensive, high in protein, and healthful. Sample some 'roo at Elizabeth Quay's Balthazar restaurant or the Little Creatures Brewery in Fremantle, where they also serve barramundi fishcakes. While the cuisine at Wildflower changes seasonally, kangaroo and other local fare are often offered.

Dumpling

The center of the Chinese community in Perth is Northbridge's Roe Street. Some of the greatest Chinese cuisines outside of Asia can be found here, including dim sum brunch or yum cha.

With lines forming around the block on weekends, Authentic Bites Dumpling House in Northbridge is the current king of Perth's dumpling scene. However, Shy John's elevates things even further with its unique combination of brewery and dim sum idea.

Lamb

Due to the state's long history of sheep farming, lamb is a staple of Western Australian cuisine. For a large portion of the 19th century, wool was Australia's most significant export, and the prosperity of the nation is sometimes referred to as "riding on the sheep's back."

There are a gazillion ways to eat lamb in Perth. With its lamb skewers, chargrilled lamb shanks, and lamb burgers, Hey Griller is a carnivore's paradise located in Victoria Park. The Fluffy Lamb at the Fremantle Markets offers charcoal-grilled lamb with an Indonesian twist.

TOP RESTAURANTS

COOGEE COMMON

Where: Coogee, 371 Cockburn Road

Common Coogee, like its well-known sister eatery Bread in Common, is everything from "common." Restored to its former glory, this 120-year-old location now houses a quaint cafe with a vibrant garden full of seasonal food. Head Chef Scott Brannigan's menu features a delectable array of carefully crafted meals that showcase the daily selections from the on-site garden. Imagine delicious green salads, mead brewed with locally sourced honey, and homemade drinks to wash it all down. It is the epitome of ethical cuisine. Enjoy a two-course lunch and beverages while taking a tour of the garden to see it all for yourself.

LE REBELLE

Where: Mount Lawley, 676 Beaufort St.

Le Rebelle is a charming neighborhood hangout renowned for its cozy interiors and old-world romanticism of Paris and New York restaurants. If romance is on the agenda, you won't be disappointed. Le Rebelle is a fantastic venue for a romantic evening, offering a delightful selection of European and Australian wines to enjoy in between delectable servings of contemporary classic cuisine. Choose your favorite among the three levels of the restaurant, each offering a unique atmosphere to fit your mood.

WILDFLOWER

Where: Perth, Level 4, 1 Cathedral Ave.

Delicious Native ingredients combine with exquisite cuisine and breathtaking vistas. Look no further if you're searching for a distinctive special occasion location in Perth. Forager-driven meals are elevated to a whole new level at the acclaimed Wildflower restaurant. This charming rooftop restaurant serves fresh local cuisine in a simple, creative style, celebrating the six of the Indigenous Noongar calendar in addition to the four seasons. When dining here, you can expect to be astounded by innovative delicacies as you take in a broad panorama of Perth and the Swan River.

LONG CHIM

Where: Barrack Street and St. Georges Terrace in Perth's State buildings

Australian chef David Thompson brings the vivid flavors and pulsating energy of Bangkok to the center of Perth's historic streets. In a vibrant restaurant setting with exposed brick walls and humorous graffiti, Long Chim dishes customers fresh, genuine flavors inspired by

Thailand's market food booths. The name translates to "come and taste" in Thai, and your taste buds will thank you for it.

Woodfire Kitchen Manuka
Where: Fremantle, 134 High St.

The place to go for comfort cuisine en masse is Manuka Woodfire Kitchen. Under the direction of the renowned Kenny McHardy, the cuisine varies according to the season, but fire is a staple of this little kitchen that never goes out of style. A feast for the senses, the menu features everything from crispy chicken to smokey beetroots and wood-fired pizza. Enjoy it with regional favorites, such as wines and beers from Western Australia and Margaret River.

TIGERS AND LIONS
Where: Fremantle, 8 Bannister St.

The Lions and Tigers, an Anglo-Indian-inspired restaurant in the center of Fremantle, originated from the founders of the popular breakfast spot Duck Duck Bruce. Filled with positive energy, intriguing tastes, and fresh seasonal ingredients, Lions and Tigers blend the essence of Australia with fine Indian cuisine. In the capital of Western Australia, it's a unique experience, so if you're seeking something hot, make reservations in advance and prepare to indulge your palate.

COFFEE SHOPS AND CAFES

1. Hylin
This café, inspired by New York City, is a must-see. In addition to providing locally sourced furnishings, artwork, and delicious cuisine, this coffee shop in Perth also sources its beans from Micrology Coffee, an independent local roaster. People are waiting outside the door for the coffee, and the all-day menu includes items like an all-

day New Yorker Reuben bagel, açaí bowls, and even crumpets that are fresh from the neighborhood farmers' market. Is there anything not to love?
178 Railway Parade, West Leederville, 6007 is the address.
Contact number: 0476 644 997
Hours: Sun 7:30 am – 2:30 pm, Mon-Sat 6:30 am-3 pm

2. Coffee La Veen

Nestled inside a historic structure with a faded façade, this café is maybe the greatest in all of Perth. You are providing a range of beans from Rockingham's Five Senses in addition to other bean varieties obtained from small roasters, most of whom are located in the east. You would be a fool not to go, with knowledgeable staff members who love teaching guests about different brewing processes and delicious meals from casual dining to something more sophisticated!
90 King Street, Perth 6000 is the address.
Contact number: 9321 1188
Hours: Sat-Sun 7:30 am – 2:00 pm, Mon–Fri 6:30 am–3 pm

3. Grouch and Co

Grouch & Co. gets its beans from global single-origin farms, varying their mixes according to the season. The beans are roasted in-house and have a distinct flavor thanks to the option of cashew or full cream milk. Not to mention teas, all of which are served in beautifully crafted ceramic cups created by Japanese artist Naomi Sugi, who is living in Washington.
Address: Myaree 6154, 1, 45 McCoy Street
Call 08 9317 1951.
Hours: 6:30 am–3 pm, Monday–Friday

4. Felix & Co

Felix & Co., one of the list's most eclectic cafés, takes its coffee seriously. You're really spoilt for choice, with many guest seasonal blends available every week, including three espresso options and two daily cold-brew options. Still more, though: Proud Mary, Dukes, Loaded, Mano a Mano, the Gordon Street Garage's in-house roastery, Small Batch, Seven Seeds, Code Black, and Market Lane are among the beans that are sourced. To say that Artificer, Mecca Espresso, Sample, and Single O are sources of coffee from New South Wales is an understatement. This is a destination for coffee lovers.

The address is 160 Hampden Road, Shop 8, Nedlands 6009
Call 08 9386 9775.
Hours: Saturday–Sun 7 am–1 pm; Monday–Friday 6:30 am–3 pm

5. Espresso Engine Room

Engine Room Espresso won't let you down, whether you choose to try the house blend or the single-origin bean of the month from the WA boutique roastery. The crew, who operate one of the greatest coffee shops in Perth, serves delicious pumpkin bread, organic crumpets, real bagels from The Holy Bagel Co., and granola or muesli breakfast cups that can be taken out.

Address: North Perth 6006, 450C Fitzgerald Street
Hours: Saturday–Sun 7 am–2 pm; Mon–Fri 6:30 am–2 pm

FOOD MARKETS

Old Shanghai

Speaking about Perth's hawkers markets would be incomplete without mentioning Old Shanghai, a decades-old landmark in the city. Look no further than Northbridge's very own Old Shanghai if you're yearning for a taste of busy crowds and quick-witted chefs dishing out delectable, genuine Asian food at La Singaporean marketplaces. With a community eating space at its heart, Old Shanghai follows the practice of bringing together a variety of vendors in one place, serving up popular favorites like Yum Cha, traditional Malaysian food, and even American-style burgers.

The Night Markets at Inglewood

Visiting a hawker market might be the ideal solution if you detest having to cook on Monday evenings after work and you're searching for something more filling than a fast drive-through. The Inglewood Night Markets, which are open every Monday, provide easy takeout choices from a variety of food trucks. Cooking at home is a vibrant (and more social) alternative to this busy (and dog-friendly) place with live entertainment, boutique shopping booths, and coffee-to-go. Before they close for the season on March 29, be sure to take full advantage of this well-liked night market, which ends on that day.

Sunset Markets in Scarborough
Ever since its debut in 2018, the Scarborough Sunset Markets have brought some vibrancy to the Scarborough beachfront by returning every year in the summer and winter. It's a terrific place for a Thursday night family adventure, with a range of vendors providing fresh food, drinks, and handmade artisanal things for guests to peruse. When you combine this with the amazing weekly acts that play locally and the breathtaking setting just by the beach, you can see how Scarborough Sunset Market offers an Australian alternative to the classic hawkers' market.

The Twilight Food Market
The largest street food market in the city is getting ready to open again for the summer.
Each Friday after work, indulge your palate with a range of reasonably priced international cuisines, showcasing Perth's rich culinary culture. During the warmer months, the pleasant weather will make you feel like you are enjoying delicious food, lively entertainment, and a twilight exploration of our lovely city.
From 4:30 p.m., food is provided.

SHOPPING IN PERTH

SHOPPING DISTRICTS AND STREETS

Shopping Destinations in Perth City

Discover the most popular retail locations in Perth City right here in the center of Perth CBD.

Get the inside scoop on the city's retail resurgence, which has seen the arrival of distinctive boutiques, antique shops, and surprising fashion collaboration spaces alongside brand-new businesses and well-known names.

King Street

King Street is located on the western edge of the city. This cobblestone street, which has been around for more than 150 years, is surrounded by lovely historic houses and a variety of interesting shops.

Premium jeweler Linneys may be found here at Kookai and Cult Status stores.

King St Collective, which has an ever-changing inventory and is a fervent promoter of WA's locally manufactured items, is located across the street.

Whereabouts
King Street
Perth, Western Australia 6000

Square Raine

In the center of Perth, Raine Square is now the city's main hub for eating, shopping, and entertainment after a significant makeover.

Raine Square, which is directly adjacent to the Underground Train Station, is a visual treat, artfully fusing the heritage-listed 1883 The Royal Hotel with a contemporary gold façade.

With its selection of Chanel, Louis Vuitton, Tiffany & Co., Kailis Jewellery, Cabinet Noir, and Swiss watches, Raine Square is a haven for those who appreciate better things in life.

Palace Cinema is the perfect diversion when your feet are screaming for a rest after a long day of shopping. The single movie theater in the city, Palace Raine Square, provides an abundant cinematic experience, complete with in-theater wait service from the wide selection of food choices in the center below.

Whereabouts
Murray Street, 300

Perth, Western Australia 6000

Watertown Brand Outlet

If you want to browse for the greatest deals around, go to Watertown, which is just a 15-minute walk or a short Yellow CAT ride from the city center.

It's worth the trip, with over 100 businesses offering clothing, accessories, gifts, home goods, athletics, and leisure.

For sports and streetwear, 2XU, Adidas, and Converse are available. For your next excursion, check out the outdoor shop Kathmandu and the footwear store Florsheim. Visit Royal Doulton and Sheridan, and you'll thank yourself and your house (as well as your checkbook) for the huge discounts on brands like Decjuba, Levi's, and Seed.

A variety of eateries and lunch alternatives are available to keep you going throughout the day. You'll need to do a few loops around Watertown to ensure you don't miss a deal since this is a marathon rather than a sprint!

Whereabouts
Wellington Street, 840
Perth, West 6005

Brookfield Place

One of the most important business districts in Australia, Brookfield Place, is paving the way for a bright future.

Situated in the center of the Perth CBD, the area seamlessly blends top-notch architecture and modern facilities.

There are a lot of retail stores and eateries at Brookfield Place.

Whereabouts
St. Georges Terrace, 125
Perth, Western Australia 6000

MALLS AND SHOPPING CENTERS

The Westfield Carousel
Large and bustling is the Westfield Carousel retail center. Its wide variety of stores makes getting lost simply in case you forget your way. Along with being exceedingly clean, the mall offers many dining and drinking options. When the weather is pleasant, it's a terrific area to go shopping.

Fremantle Markets
Founded in 1897, Fremantle Markets is a thriving indoor market. It has a range of booths offering handicrafts, local goods, clothing, and cuisine. Situated at the confluence of the Swan River and the Indian Ocean, Fremantle is a bustling port city renowned for its bountiful markets and quaint ambiance. The markets are a riot of color and energy, drawing crowds with their eye-catching exhibits.

The shopping center Karrinyup
The spacious Karrinyup Shopping Centre, which has high ceilings and an array of stores and eateries, is a well-liked destination for residents. It's a great area to spend a day since it has restaurants and movie theaters.

Whitford City Westfield
In Perth, Western Australia, there is a sizable and well-liked retail center called Westfield Whitford City. Kmart, Big W, Woolworths, Peter Alexander, Jamaica Blue Pharmacy, and many more retailers are among its many offerings. In addition, the mall has an outdoor space with play areas and kid-friendly equipment.
Joondalup Shopping City by the Lake

The large retail center includes more than 300 retailers, a theater, two food courts, and outdoor dining options.

ABORIGINAL ART AND SOUVENIRS

Aboriginal art
Because of its distinctive style and wide range of aesthetics, Aboriginal artworks and artifacts have been a major export from the nation since the British colonized the area over 30,000 years ago. Because of this, out of all the Perth souvenirs, this is the one to think of giving.

Some items could be more appropriate for a traveler wanting to breeze through customs. Still, a didgeridoo might be a bit difficult to get on the aircraft (but we don't discourage you from bringing this back since it makes a wonderful present). Printmaking, textile art, paintings, weavings, sculpture, and rock carvings are all excellent keepsakes from Perth that honor Australia's rich and priceless Aboriginal past.

Visit these Perth souvenir stores to see some amazing, unique artwork:

Gallery Japingka. 47 on the High Street. Opens at ten in the morning.

Perth's Creative Natives. 58th Street, Forest Chase. Opens at ten in the morning.

The breath of the digeridoo. Market Street No. 6. Starts at 10:30

Beach Styles
Nothing says "Aussie" quite like tanned skin, a freshly used surfboard, and a bikini tan. What should you gift your girlfriends in Perth? One can never have too many bathing suits. Make sure you pick up the

beachwear that is almost as well-known as the large waves when you visit Cottesloe Beach.

You'll stand out at whatever resort you visit once you return home since swimwear companies like Seafolly, Zimmermann Wear, and White Sand Australia are more stylish than American faves like Billabong and Oakley. Beachwear presents are fantastic keepsakes from Perth that are useful in addition to being amazing.

Antiques

Searching around the tourist stores in Perth for antiques is perhaps one of the more unusual things to do there. The easiest way to change that, even if Perth may not be well-known worldwide, is to go at the enormous assortment of retro Perth souvenirs that are offered. On a gloomy day or as the centerpiece of your vacation, the souvenir stores in Perth have enough to keep you entertained, from local music recordings and apparel to fishing gear and fantastic furniture discoveries. The major attraction of these thrift stores is the opportunity to interact closely with the products; the meticulously curated selections emphasize detail, so take your time looking over each item. Antiques should unquestionably be on your list of things to purchase in Perth.

Visit these souvenir stores in Perth to make your discoveries of wonderful items:

Curio Warehouse. James St., Guildford, 141. opens at ten thirty in the morning.

Vintage Bluebird. Cambridge Street, Wemberley, 288. opens at ten in the morning.

Effies Guildford Emporium. Guildford's James Street, 141. opens at ten thirty in the morning.

Record Fat Shan. 37 Barrack St. The Basement. Opens at ten in the morning.

Wine

With a vast variety of excellent wines produced by the vineyards, Swan Valley is one of Perth's most popular tourist attractions. Bringing home a fine bottle of wine, whether it's a dark red or white, is a wonderful way to treat the neighbors, make an impression on the employer, or surprise a loved one. Thus, be sure to pack the pleasure for later and enjoy the full-day vineyard excursions as well.

Check out these vineyards, even if they're not on your trip itinerary:

Vine Ugly Ducklings. 11:00 am 7790 W Swan Rd. Shiraz liqueur is the best buy.

The Vineyard of Tyler. 11:00 am, 301 Padbury Ave. Red Grenache 2014 is the best buy.

Swan Valley Winery Coward & Black. 9 a.m. at 448 Harmans Mill Road. Semillion Sauvignon Blanc is the best deal.

Quokka

Put aside koalas and kangaroos; there's a new Aussie favorite in town. This adorable little cuddle bug would make any animal lover shout with delight, so you really must bring one home. There doesn't appear to be any damage in a stuffed animal version of the quokka making its way from the toy shop to the arms of friends and family back home, even if this is by no means an endorsement to get a real quokka before departing Oz.

When visiting Perth with children, a quokka is sure to become their new best friend. These little Wallabies are adorable and resemble a cross between a kangaroo and a mouse. Visit the Perth Zoo to see these cute animals, then make your way to the gift store to pick up one for the trip home. This soft plush animal is a terrific choice for a Perth gift, and it's available at most souvenir stores in the city.

ENTERTAINMENT AND NIGHTLIFE

BARS, PUBS AND CLUBS

Toots

Location: Northbridge

Toots is a disco dance club in Northbridge that is concealed in plain sight, a hidden bar WITHIN a secret bar. It would help if you first located Sneaky Tony's, the underground speakeasy pub tucked away in a Chinatown back alley, to find Toots. The password will then need to be known, so ask the bartender, "Is Toots in? for entry. Once inside, anticipate lots of disco balls, vintage drinks (Appletini, anyone?), and music from the 1970s.

Si paradiso

Location: Highgate

This beautiful retro-Italian venue offers nonstop dancing, drinking, and eating for a great time. Combining elements of an amphitheater, cocktail bar, and underground dance club, the latter is home to some of Perth's top DJs and frequent performances by talented interstate DJs who spark up a frenzy on the dance floor. Join us for a Sunday brunch à la carte, including $2 oysters, drink carafes, pizza deals, and DJs playing Paradiso music.

Barbes

Location: East Perth

Barbes is the perfect place to be if you're searching for mind-bending sounds and boiler room vibes. Different evenings include anything from old-school hip hop and afro rhythms to thundering electronica and techno. The club draws some of the greatest DJs from all around.

Connections

Location: Northbridge

Perth's nightlife is incomplete without Connections, which is said to be the longest-running homosexual club in the southern hemisphere. The LGBTQIA+ community has had a haven there since 1975. Check out Connections' Facebook page to see what's happening. From drag performances by Perth's most skilled queens to midweek "Bingay" nights with international DJs, there's something for everyone.

Purple

Location: Leederville

Purple is Leederville's late-night pub and club, offering party vibes every Saturday night till the wee hours of Sunday morning in the area that once housed The Manor. With weekend performances by both

local and traveling musicians, Purple is mostly focused on electronic music, in contrast to its predecessor, which was primarily a
hip-hop bar.

The Rechabite
Location: Northbridge
This multi-story playhouse has a rooftop bar, restaurant, theater, and basement bar. And every weekend, there are a ton of events going on across the facility because of all that room. The environment in The Rechabite is very inclusive and always fun, with everything from the hippest live performances in the massive historical hall to the dirtiest DJ takeovers in the dungeon-like Goodwill Basement Club.

The old Synagog
Fremantle
Known affectionately as The 'Gog, this beloved Freo location is the site of The Arbor, a multi-level bar that embraces and promotes cutting shapes on the dance floor. There's tap-poured beer on the rooftop terrace, gourmet pub fare served in the beer garden, and a dedicated dance area below. You'll know you've arrived at The Abor's underground dancing area, "the naughty corner," when you see the blazing neon sign.

Magnet House
Perth Central Business District
It would be impossible to discuss Perth clubs without mentioning Maggies. With VIP booths, many rooms, weekly party nights, and plenty of neon lights, it's your typical big club experience. They also have an amazing LED light system above the dance floor that dances to the music and will blow your mind. You may always go to their link

club, Amplifier, for a dance and a bowl on their on-site alley for more classic rock and indie vibes.

LIVE MUSIC AND PERFORMANCE VENUES

- The Rechabite in Northbridge is unique because of its multi-level complex that combines a variety of eating and entertainment options. This renovated venue promises a wide variety of live music events.
- Jack Rabbit Slim's presents a distinctive fusion of live music venue and 1950s restaurant, a la Pulp Fiction. It's well-known for showcasing a broad range of musical styles and is a well-liked location for both residents and tourists.
- Housed in the refurbished former Drill Hall, Freo. Social in Fremantle has swiftly gained popularity. It has a cutting-edge sound system, seating for up to 550 people, and a dynamic program of music, food, and beverages.

Cinemas & Theaters:
1. A historic theater that hosts a combination of live music and film is Mount Lawley's Astor Theatre. This grand art deco building presents a variety of performances and cinematic experiences by gifted regional, national, and worldwide artists.

ZXDFGHjklOne of Perth's most recognizable theaters, His Majesty's Theatre presents a variety of shows, including comedy, contemporary music, and ballet and opera. The location itself is a stunning illustration of Edwardian Baroque building design.

FAMILY-FRIENDLY ACTIVITIES

1. In addition to being a verdant haven, Kings Park and Botanic Garden is also the location of a number of kid-friendly playgrounds, such as the Rio Tinto Naturescape, which inspires children to interact with the natural world. The park is ideal for a family outing since it has a variety of picnic sites with grills.

2. The Perth Mint: Visitors of all ages may experience the wonder of gold here thanks to a special combination of displays, demonstrations, and activities. The whole family will enjoy this instructive and fun event.

3. Jump, flip, and play dodgeball at Bounce Inc., an indoor trampoline park perfect for kids and adults alike. It's an exhilarating family activity with locations in Cannington and Joondalup.

4. Explore the animal world and get up close and personal with your favorite creatures at Perth Zoo. To make the most of your visit, the zoo offers a variety of suggested itineraries for either a half-day or full-day excursion.

5. Elizabeth Quay: Art, exhibits, dining options, cafés, boat cruises, and playgrounds can all be found in this waterfront entertainment district. Highlights include the opportunity to climb the Bell Tower for sweeping views over Perth and the Venetian carousel.

6. Caversham Animal Park: Just a short drive from Perth, this park offers an all-encompassing Australian animal experience, complete with interactive displays, seeing wombats and koalas, and feeding kangaroos.

7. Escape rooms are a thrilling and difficult pastime with a range of family-friendly themes. Several noteworthy ones include Time's Up in Wanneroo and Bunbury, which offers both indoor and outdoor

adventures, and Escape Hunt in Fremantle, which has chambers with a Disney theme.

8. Natural Swimming Spots: Lake Leschenaultia in Chidlow and other similar locations provide serene waters that are perfect for swimming and canoeing in a natural environment for people seeking to get away from the city.

9. Penguin Island: From Rockingham, take a short boat ride to get to know some of Perth's cutest citizens—the adorable penguins. The island has stunning beaches and a variety of animal encounters.

10. Scitech: This scientific museum is a fun and instructive family adventure that features interactive displays, puppet performances, live science experiments, and stargazing sessions.

OUTDOOR ADVENTURES AND ACTIVITIES

PARKS AND GARDENS

Perth is a beautiful city that has an abundance of colorful parks and gardens that provide a never-ending list of things to see and do.

There are lots of friendly spots to people-watch, whether you're strolling through Kings Park & Botanic Garden's wildflowers or snapping a photo in front of Stirling Gardens' kangaroo sculptures on St Georges Terrace.

There are also many parks and reserves where you can play football, let the kids run about, or have a leisurely picnic.

Claisebrook

This urban park, which was created in the 1990s as a component of Claisebrook Cove Village, has grass and natural wetlands in addition to covered areas for strolling.

Additionally, artwork depicting East Perth's natural wetland condition and the ability of water to modify the environment may be found in a central "channel."

The waterway enters and exits the lake, supplying enough water to irrigate around ten hectares of parklands in East Perth, all the while serving as a decorative element for the reserve.

The lakes get their water from the Claisebrook storm water drain, where the canal finishes at Claisebrook Cove.

Additionally, underpasses provide secure access across the path to Claisebrook Cove, home to a number of eateries with lake views and cafés.

Whereabouts
The easternmost portion of Royal Street
Perth East, WA 600

Gardens at Council House

The Council's administrative buildings have a formal exterior thanks to these lovely gardens in the heart of Perth City, which also draw attention to the building's historic listing.
Following Council House's 1999 renovation, the present-day Council House Gardens were created.
Many of the 1860s-era trees were kept throughout the renovation, and most of the gardens are situated on the roof of an underground parking garage.
In the CBD, the garden is the ideal place to spend some peaceful time introspecting.
Whereabouts
St Georges Terrace 27,
Perth, Western Australia 6000

Gardens of Harold Boas

This stunning inner-city park has a tranquil lake, a waterfall, and a rock cascade.
The gardens, which include a lake, waterfall, and rock cascade in honor of architect and former City of Perth Councillor Harold Boas, are named after him.
Harold Boas offers city workers a tranquil escape with its vast grassy spaces and plenty of shade from the mature trees.
Once called Delhi Square, the park underwent renovations in 1976, preserving many of the ancient trees that had been planted there in 1900.

With four spaces designated for wedding ceremonies, the gardens are a well-liked venue for bridal parties.
Whereabouts
Havelock Street and Wellington
Perth, West 6005

Abrahams Reserve by JH

JH Abrahams Reserve is a well-liked venue for picnics and recreational activities. It has large, grassy, shaded sections with picnic tables and play equipment.

The Reserve, sometimes called Pelican Point, is a well-liked off-leash dog exercise facility situated between the Nedlands Yacht Club and Matilda Bay Reserve.

Significant conservation importance may also be found at JH Abrahams Reserve.

The Reserve, which serves as a hub for citywide leisure activities, is a fantastic spot for bike rides and outdoor games with the kids while enjoying breathtaking views of the river.

Whereabouts
Drive Hackett
WA 6009 Crawley

Kings Park

A short walk from Perth's city center, 400 hectares of towering trees, breathtaking woodlands, lakes, landscaped gardens, and picnic spaces can be found right in the city.

When in Perth's west end, you must see the King of All Parks. More than six kid-friendly play places can be found in Kings Park Botanic Garden, including Saw Avenue Picnic Area, DNA Tower, Lotterywest Family Area, Ivey Watson Playground, Synergy Parkland (Dinosaur

Playground), and Variety Place, to mention a few. Along with a large number of eateries, the park has restrooms, changing places, and BBQ areas. Additionally, you may monitor the many educational activities that Kings Park provides for children of all ages.

A natural paradise, Kings Park is home to the magnificent Western Australian Botanic Garden. It is replete with jogging and walking paths bordered by native flora, blooming wildflowers, and a rich Aboriginal past.

The ideal time to see the nearly 3,000 distinct types of wildflowers on show at Kings Park is during the September Kings Park Festival (see the video below for more information). Experience thousands of Western Australian wildflowers in full bloom together with a plethora of amazing free events, including presentations, guided walks, family activities, and exhibits.

Whereabouts

Fraser Street

Perth, Western Australia 6000

The Totterdell Park

The quaint Totterdell Park is tucked away in West Perth, between the business towers.

The park, which is little but picture-perfect, is named after Sir Joseph Totterdell, who served as Perth's Lord Mayor from 1946 to 1953. Shrubbery encircles the park, creating a peaceful haven for locals and office workers to unwind in.

A big metal play frame with slides, climbing nets, ramps, monkey bars, and a climbing wall is part of the playground's soft fall play area.

The grassed area provides plenty of room for youngsters to play football and for setting up a picnic blanket to have a catch-up with friends and family.

Dogs are permitted to run free at Totterdell Park as well.
Whereabouts
Arthur Street
Perth, West 6005

HIKING AND BIKING TRAILS

Perth is the perfect place for hiking and biking because of its stunning natural surroundings:
- Eagle View Walk route: This John Forrest National Park route provides beautiful vistas as well as an opportunity to see native animals and wildflowers. This fairly difficult route is ideal for anyone who likes to spend time in the great outdoors.
- Whistlepipe Gully: A short, dog-friendly trek with lovely views of cascading water and many wildflowers. It's a fantastic option for those searching for a stroll or families.
- Lesmurdie Falls: Known for its breathtaking falls and picturesque vistas, this location offers a variety of hikes suitable for varying degrees of athleticism. It's a great place to take pictures and take in the splendor of the Perth Hills.

WATER SPORTS AND BEACH ACTIVITIES

There are several options for beach and water sports around Perth's riverbanks and coastline:
- Swimming and Surfing: Cottesloe Beach and Scarborough Beach are two of the most popular beaches in Perth for family vacations and surfing due to their gorgeous sand and crystal blue seas.

- Kayaking and Stand-Up Paddleboarding: The Swan River and its beach provide ideal conditions for these water sports, which give visitors a distinctive viewpoint of the city and its environs.

WILDLIFE ENCOUNTERS

There are many different animal encounters in Perth and its surroundings.

- Penguin Island: Only a short boat journey from Rockingham, Penguin Island offers an excellent opportunity to see young penguins living in their native environment. Families will enjoy seeing the lovely beaches and boardwalks on this fun day excursion.

- Caversham Animals Park: This Swan Valley attraction offers a fun and informative experience for visitors of all ages by letting you get up close and personal with Australian animals, such as kangaroos, koalas, and wombats.

DAY TRIPS FROM PERTH

PINNACLES DESERT

Located within Nambung National Park, approximately 200 kilometers north of Perth, the Pinnacles Desert is famous for its thousands of tall limestone spires that rise mysteriously from the yellow sands.

Getting There:
The journey to the Pinnacles begins with a scenic drive along the Indian Ocean Drive, which offers breathtaking views of the turquoise coast. The trip takes about 2 to 2.5 hours, making it a perfect destination for a day trip from Perth. Renting a car or joining an organized tour are the most common ways to visit the Pinnacles.

What to Expect:
Upon arriving at Nambung National Park, visitors can explore the Pinnacles Desert by walking around the designated paths or driving through the four-kilometer loop that winds its way through the dramatic limestone formations. These formations, some standing as high as 3.5 meters, create an almost alien landscape that photographers and nature enthusiasts love.

Other Attractions:
Besides the Pinnacles themselves, Nambung National Park is home to beautiful beaches, such as Hangover Bay and Kangaroo Point, offering opportunities for swimming, fishing, and snorkeling. The park also features a variety of flora and fauna, with spring bringing a vibrant display of wildflowers. The Pinnacles Desert Discovery Centre

provides insights into the geological processes that formed the Pinnacles and the cultural history of the area.

Best Time to Visit:
The Pinnacles Desert is accessible year-round, but the best time to visit is during the cooler months from May to October, when the weather is more comfortable for exploring. Visiting at sunrise or sunset offers the most dramatic lighting for photographs, with the low sun casting long shadows and illuminating the limestone formations.

SWAN VALLEY: WINERIES AND WILDLIFE PARKS

Getting There:
The journey to Swan Valley begins with a mere 25-minute drive northeast of Perth, making it an easily accessible destination for a day trip. Visitors can opt to drive themselves, join an organized tour, or even take a scenic cruise along the Swan River to reach the valley.

Wineries and Tastings:
Swan Valley is renowned for its warm climate wines, including Chenin Blanc, Verdelho, Shiraz, and Cabernet Sauvignon. The region is dotted with over 40 wineries, ranging from small, family-run operations to large, well-known producers. Many of these offer cellar-door tastings and vineyard tours, providing insight into the winemaking process and the opportunity to sample a variety of wines. Don't miss the chance to visit some of the boutique wineries where you can meet the winemakers and enjoy a more personal tasting experience.

Gourmet Delights:
Beyond wine, Swan Valley is a treasure trove of culinary delights. The region boasts numerous artisanal food producers, offering everything from fresh local produce to gourmet cheeses, chocolates, and honey. Several wineries also have onsite restaurants where you can enjoy a meal paired with their wines. For a unique experience, follow the Swan Valley Food and Wine Trail, a 32-kilometer loop that guides visitors through some of the region's best food and wine offerings.

Wildlife Parks:
A visit to Swan Valley wouldn't be complete without experiencing its wildlife. Caversham Wildlife Park, one of the area's top attractions, provides a chance to get up close with Australian animals such as kangaroos, koalas, wombats, and various bird species. The park offers interactive experiences, including koala photo opportunities and the chance to hand-feed kangaroos, making it a hit with families and animal lovers.

Cultural Attractions:
For those interested in local culture and history, the region's rich indigenous heritage and European settlement history are showcased in various galleries, museums, and Aboriginal tours. Exploring these can add a meaningful dimension to your Swan Valley day trip.

Best Time to Visit:
Swan Valley is a year-round destination, with each season offering its charm. Spring (September to November) is particularly lovely for visiting wineries and wildlife parks, as the weather is pleasant and the landscape is vibrant with wildflowers.

MARGARET RIVER: WINE, SURF AND CAVES

A day trip from Perth to Margaret River promises an exciting blend of wine, surf, and exploration through its enchanting caves, making it a must-visit destination for travelers seeking a taste of Western Australia's diverse offerings.

Starting the journey early from Perth, the drive to Margaret River takes approximately three hours, offering scenic views of the Western Australian coastline along the way. Upon arrival, the first stop for many is the region's renowned wineries. Margaret River is celebrated for producing over 20% of Australia's premium wine, including exceptional Cabernet Sauvignon, Chardonnay, Semillon, and Sauvignon Blanc. A guided wine tasting at one of the boutique wineries offers an intimate glimpse into the winemaking process, accompanied by the opportunity to savor some of the finest vintages.

After indulging in the local flavors, the adventure continues to the coast, where Margaret River's surf breaks are legendary among surfing enthusiasts. Even if you're not keen on surfing, watching the surfers tackle the waves at spots like Surfers Point and Prevelly is a thrilling experience. The region's beaches also provide a serene backdrop for a leisurely lunch or a stroll along the pristine sands, with the Indian Ocean's vast expanse stretching out before you.

The final highlight of the day trip is exploring Margaret River's ancient limestone caves. These natural wonders, formed thousands of years ago, lie beneath the Leeuwin Naturaliste Ridge. Guided tours are available for caves like Mammoth Cave, Lake Cave, and Jewel Cave, each offering unique formations such as stalactites, stalagmites, and crystal formations. Lake Cave, for example, is a stunning crystal chamber deep beneath the earth, where reflections on the water's surface create a mesmerizing, mirror-like illusion.

NATIONAL PARKS AND NATURAL WONDERS

The day begins with an early departure from Perth, heading towards one of the many national parks that dot the region. A popular choice is Yanchep National Park, located approximately an hour's drive north of Perth. This park is renowned for its koala-viewing boardwalk, where visitors can spot these adorable creatures in their natural habitat. Yanchep also boasts a network of walking trails that meander through its stunning bushland, wetlands, and coastal plain ecosystems. It offers a chance to observe the area's rich biodiversity, including kangaroos, native birds, and an array of plant species.

Another must-visit destination is the Pinnacles Desert in Nambung National Park, around two hours drive northwest of Perth. This remarkable landscape features thousands of limestone spires rising eerily from the yellow sands, creating a surreal, moon-like surface that captivates visitors. The Pinnacles can be explored by walking trails or by driving along the scenic loop. This area also offers the opportunity to visit the nearby pristine beaches and the vibrant fishing town of Cervantes, known for its fresh seafood.

For those willing to venture further, the Margaret River region, while more famous for its wine, also offers access to the Leeuwin-Naturaliste National Park, where the natural limestone caves and coastal walks present another facet of Western Australia's diverse natural beauty. Although a full exploration of Margaret River might be ambitious for a single-day trip, it's possible to combine a cave visit with scenic stops along the coastline.

Closer to Perth, Serpentine National Park offers the spectacular Serpentine Falls, a serene spot for picnicking and swimming in the natural pools beneath the cascading waters. The park's numerous trails cater to all levels of hikers, providing scenic views of the falls, the Serpentine River, and the surrounding forest.

No day trip from Perth into its surrounding natural wonders would be complete without acknowledging the importance of conservation and the role visitors play in preserving these pristine environments for future generations. Practices such as adhering to designated trails, taking all rubbish with you, and respecting wildlife habitats contribute to the sustainability of these magnificent sites.

Returning to Perth after a day of
exploration, visitors carry with them a deeper appreciation for Western Australia's natural beauty and the unforgettable memories of their encounters with the wilderness.

PRACTICAL INFORMATION FOR TRAVELERS

VISA AND ENTRY REQUIREMENTS

Travelers to Perth from overseas will need to apply for an Australian visa ahead of their journey. The type of visa required depends on your nationality, the purpose of your visit, and how long you plan to stay. Tourists can typically apply for an Electronic Travel Authority (ETA) or an eVisitor visa, both of which are linked electronically to their passports. It's crucial to check the Australian Department of Home Affairs website for the most current visa information and to apply well in advance of your trip.

HEALTH AND SAFETY TIPS

Australia is known for its high standards of health and safety, but visitors should still take precautions. Sun protection is a must, as the Australian sun is particularly strong. Wear high-SPF sunscreen, a hat, and UV-protective clothing. If you're going to be exploring Perth's natural beauty, be mindful of water safety at beaches and stay informed about any bushfire warnings in the summer months. It's also wise to have comprehensive travel insurance that covers medical expenses.

CURRENCY, BANKING AND TIPPING

The Australian Dollar (AUD) is the currency used in Perth. Credit and debit cards are widely accepted, and ATMs are readily available. While tipping is not as customary in Australia as in some other countries, it is appreciated for exceptional service in restaurants, cafes, and taxis, with a typical tip being around 10% of the bill. In casual dining settings or bars, tipping is not expected.

LOCAL CUSTOMS AND ETIQUETTE

Australians are generally laid-back and informal, and this extends to their approach to greetings, which are typically friendly and straightforward. However, politeness is valued, and a "please" and "thank you" go a long way. When visiting beaches or public pools, it's important to swim between the red and yellow flags, which indicate a patrolled area. Australians are also very environmentally conscious, so be mindful of recycling rules and respect local wildlife and natural surroundings.

COMMUNICATION: WI-FI, SIM CARDS AND APPS

Staying connected in Perth is easy, with many cafes, restaurants, and public spaces offering free Wi-Fi. For more consistent access, consider purchasing a local SIM card upon arrival; these are available at the airport and various retailers. Australia has good mobile network coverage, especially in urban areas like Perth. To navigate the city's public transport schedules or to discover local attractions and dining options, downloading popular Australian apps like Transperth for public transport, Zomato for dining, and the Australian Bureau of Meteorology for weather forecasts can be incredibly helpful.

EMERGENCY CONTACTS

- Triple Zero (000): The primary emergency service number in Australia for police, fire, and ambulance services. It can be dialed from any phone, including mobiles, even without credit or a SIM card. When calling, be prepared to provide your location, the nature of the emergency, and your contact details.
- Non-Emergency Police Assistance: For non-urgent police assistance, dial 131 444. This number is for situations where you need police help, but there is no immediate danger.
- Poison Information Centre: For advice on poisonings, envenomations, or toxic exposures, contact the Poison Information Centre at 13 11 26, available 24/7 across Australia.
- Medical Services
- Healthdirect Australia: For non-emergency health advice, Healthdirect offers a 24/7 hotline at 1800 022 222, where you can speak to a registered nurse about health concerns.
- Hospitals: Perth has several major hospitals equipped with emergency departments, including Royal Perth Hospital (+61 8 9224 2244) and Sir Charles Gairdner Hospital (+61 8 6457 3333).
- Other Useful Contacts
- State Emergency Service (SES): For emergency assistance during floods, storms, or natural disasters, contact the SES at 132 500.
- Consulates and Embassies: Depending on your nationality, it may be useful to have the contact details of your country's consulate or embassy in case of lost passports or other legal issues. The Australian Department of Foreign Affairs and Trade website lists foreign embassies and consulates in Australia.

CONCLUSION

As we draw the curtain on this comprehensive journey through the vibrant heart and soul of Perth, it's hard not to feel a profound connection to the land, its culture, and its people. Our adventure, chronicled in these pages, has been a mosaic of unforgettable moments—from the serene beauty of Kings Park at sunrise to the lively hum of Fremantle Markets at noon and the majestic sunsets over Cottesloe Beach.

Each chapter was crafted to not only guide but to inspire—to create an emotional bond with places both iconic and hidden, weaving a narrative that celebrates Perth's unique essence. We've shared practical tips to navigate this splendid city with ease, from savoring its culinary delights to embracing the exhilarating outdoor lifestyle, ensuring your experience is as seamless as it is memorable.

My deepest gratitude goes to you, dear reader, for embarking on this journey with me. Your curiosity and wanderlust are what bring these words to life. As we've explored together, remember that Perth, with its endless horizons, is just the beginning of a larger story waiting to be discovered.

I encourage you to continue exploring to seek out new adventures beyond the pages of this guide. Let the vivid language of Perth's landscapes and the warmth of its people inspire you to delve deeper, travel further, and dream bigger.

Consider this not as an ending but an invitation—an invitation to step out, to experience the world with open eyes and an open heart. May you carry the spirit of Perth with you, letting it guide your steps to new horizons.

With heartfelt thanks and a dash of wanderlust,
[DANIEL C. FLICK]

Printed in Great Britain
by Amazon